Snap books ™

Fun Food for Cool Cooks

Monkey Pudding

AND OTHER DESSERT RECIPES

by Kristi Johnson

Capstone press®

Mankato, Minnesota

Snap Books are published by Capstone Press,
151 Good Counsel Drive, P.O. Box 669, Mankato, Minnesota 56002.
www.capstonepress.com

Library of Congress Cataloging-in-Publication Data
Johnson, Kristi.
    Monkey pudding and other dessert recipes / by Kristi Johnson.
    p. cm. — (Snap books. Fun food for cool cooks)
    Summary: "Provides fun and unique recipes for desserts, including cake, pecan pie, and cookies.
Includes easy instructions and a helpful tools glossary with photos" — Provided by publisher.
    Includes bibliographical references and index.
    ISBN-13: 978-1-4296-1337-8 (hardcover)
    ISBN-10: 1-4296-1337-8 (hardcover)
    1. Desserts — Juvenile literature. I. Title. II. Series.

TX773.J635 2008
641.8'6 — dc22   2007031315

Editors: Kathryn Clay and Becky Viaene
Designer: Juliette Peters
Photo Stylist: Kelly Garvin

Photo Credits:
All principle photography in this book by Capstone Press/Karon Dubke
Capstone Press/TJ Thoraldson Digital Photography, cooking utensils (all)
Tami Johnson, 32

TABLE OF CONTENTS

INTRODUCTION

SEEING STARS

When choosing a recipe, let the stars be your guide. Just follow this chart to find recipes that fit your cooking comfort level.

EASY: ★ ☆ ☆
MEDIUM: ★ ★ ☆
ADVANCED: ★ ★ ★

Who's hungry for dessert? You are! You can't wait to dig into a sweet treat. A great-tasting dessert adds a fantastic finishing touch to almost any meal.

In this book, you'll find fun and wacky dessert recipes that are easy to make and even easier to enjoy. You're sure to find a tasty treat to satisfy everyone's sweet tooth. From chocolate and cherries to ice cream and cream cheese — which one will be your favorite?

METRIC CONVERSION GUIDE

United States	Metric
¼ teaspoon	1.2 mL
½ teaspoon	2.5 mL
1 teaspoon	5 mL
1 tablespoon	15 mL
¼ cup	60 mL
⅓ cup	80 mL
½ cup	120 mL
⅔ cup	160 mL
¾ cup	175 mL
1 cup	240 mL
1 quart	1 liter
1 ounce	30 grams
2 ounces	55 grams
4 ounces	110 grams
½ pound	225 grams
1 pound	455 grams

Fahrenheit	Celsius
325°	160°
350°	180°
375°	190°
400°	200°
425°	220°
450°	230°

All good cooks know that a successful recipe takes a little preparation. Use this handy checklist to save time when working in the kitchen.

BEFORE YOU BEGIN

READ YOUR RECIPE

Once you've chosen a recipe, carefully read over it. The recipe will go smoothly if you understand the steps and techniques.

CHECK THE PANTRY

Make sure you have all the ingredients on hand. After all, it's hard to bake cookies without sugar!

DRESS FOR SUCCESS

Wear an apron to keep your clothes clean. Roll up long sleeves. Tie long hair back so it doesn't get in your way — or in the food.

GET OUT YOUR TOOLS

Sort through the cupboards and gather all the tools you'll need to prepare the recipe. Can't tell a spatula from a mixing spoon? No problem. Refer to the handy tools glossary in this book.

PREPARE YOUR INGREDIENTS

A little prep time at the start will pay off in the end.

- Rinse any fresh ingredients such as fruit and vegetables.
- Use a peeler to remove the peel from foods like apples and carrots.
- Cut up fresh ingredients as called for in the recipe. Keep an adult nearby when using a knife to cut or chop food.
- Measure all the ingredients and place them in separate bowls or containers so they're ready to use. Remember to use the correct measuring cups for dry and wet ingredients.

PREHEAT THE OVEN

If you're baking treats, it's important to preheat the oven. Cakes, cookies, and breads bake better in an oven that's heated to the correct temperature.

The kitchen may be unfamiliar turf for many young chefs. Here's a list of trusty tips to help keep you safe in the kitchen:

KITCHEN SAFETY

ADULT HELPERS

Ask an adult to help. Whether you're chopping, mixing, or baking, you'll want an adult nearby to lend a hand or answer questions.

FIRST AID

Keep a first aid kit handy in the kitchen, just in case you have an accident. A basic first aid kit contains bandages, a cream or spray to treat burns, alcohol wipes, gauze, and a small scissors.

WASH UP

Before starting any recipe, be sure to wash your hands. Wash your hands again after working with messy ingredients like jelly or syrup.

HANDLE HABITS

Turn handles of cooking pots toward the center of the stove. You don't want anyone to bump into a handle that's sticking off the stove.

USING KNIVES

It's always best to get an adult's help when using knives. Choose a knife that's the right size for both your hands and the food. It may be tough to cut carrots with paring knife that's too small. Hold the handle firmly when cutting, and keep your fingers away from the blade.

COVER UP

Always wear oven mitts or use pot holders to take hot trays and pans out of the oven.

KEEP IT CLEAN

Spills and drips are bound to happen in the kitchen. Wipe up messes with a paper towel or clean kitchen towel to keep your workspace tidy.

Monkey Pudding is a twist on banana pudding, a classic Southern favorite. With bananas and marshmallows, everyone will go ape for this tasty dessert.

MONKEY PUDDING

WHAT YOU NEED

Ingredients

2½ cups milk
1 (6-ounce) box of instant banana pudding
1 (14-ounce) can sweetened condensed milk
1 (12-ounce) container whipped topping
1 (12-ounce) package vanilla wafer cookies
2½ cups mini marshmallows
3 bananas

Tools

large mixing bowl   rubber scraper   cutting board

paring knife   small bowl

serving dish

1 In a large mixing bowl, combine milk, dry pudding mix, sweetened condensed milk, and half of the whipped topping. Stir ingredients with a rubber scraper.

2 In a serving dish, spread a layer of vanilla wafer cookies. Add 1 cup mini marshmallows on top of the cookies.

3 Peel the bananas and place them on a cutting board. Slice bananas into small pieces with a paring knife. Place half of the slices on top of the marshmallows.

4 Pour half of the pudding mixture evenly over the cookies and marshmallows.

5 Add another layer of cookies and mini marshmallows. Pour the remaining pudding mixture over the marshmallows.

6 In a small bowl, mix the remaining whipped topping with ½ cup marshmallows. Spread this mixture on top of the pudding.

7 Refrigerate overnight before serving.

My Oh My, Make It a Pie

With a few changes, you can turn this into a pie. Instead of a serving dish, use two (9-inch) prepared graham cracker pie shells. Combine milk, instant pudding, sweetened condensed milk, and half of the whipped topping. Stir in 1 cup mini marshmallows and two sliced bananas. Pour the mixture into the crusts. Top with the remaining whipped cream and ½ cup mini marshmallows. Refrigerate overnight before serving.

9

Who says pizza needs to have meat and cheese? Try adding chocolate chips and bananas to your pizza. They will soon become your favorite toppings.

DIFFICULTY LEVEL: ★ ★ ☆
SERVING SIZE: 8–10
PREHEAT OVEN: ACCORDING TO PACKAGE

CHOCOLATE CHIP BANANA PIZZA

WHAT YOU NEED

●● Ingredients

1 (3-ounce) box of instant
   vanilla pudding
1 tube refrigerated chocolate chip
   cookie dough
4-5 medium bananas
¾ cup semi-sweet chocolate chips
1 cup chocolate sauce

●● Tools

large mixing bowl   rolling mat   rolling pin

pizza pan   oven mitt   pot holder

wire cooling rack   rubber scraper   cutting board

paring knife   pizza cutter

1. In a large mixing bowl, prepare the pudding as directed on the package. Refrigerate pudding for 2 hours or until firm.

2. Put the cookie dough on the rolling mat. Use a rolling pin to flatten dough.

3. Place cookie dough onto a pizza pan. Bake dough áccording to package directions.

4. Use an oven mitt or pot holder to remove the pizza pan from the oven. Allow the crust to cool on a wire cooling rack for 15 minutes.

5. Spread the pudding onto the cooled crust with a rubber scraper.

6. Peel the bananas and place them on a cutting board. Slice bananas into thin pieces with a paring knife. Place bananas on the pudding.

7. On top of bananas, sprinkle chocolate chips. Drizzle chocolate sauce over the entire pizza.

8. Cut the pizza into slices with a pizza cutter.

Trusty Tip

It's best to make this recipe just before you want to serve it. Sliced bananas will turn brown quickly, and pudding can make the cookie pizza crust soggy. But don't worry. This dessert tastes so good, there won't be any leftovers.

It doesn't matter what the weather is like outside. Whenever you make this Sunny Fun Cake, you will think it's a hot summer day.

Sunny Fun Cake

WHAT YOU NEED

Ingredients

1 box white cake mix
1 (12-ounce) jar raspberry jam
1 (12-ounce) container whipped topping
1 (20-ounce) can sliced pineapple rings, drained
1 (10-ounce) jar maraschino cherries, drained

Tools

2 cake pans   oven mitt   pot holder

wire cooling rack   rubber scraper

nonstick cooking spray
two dinner plates

1 Spray cake pans with nonstick cooking spray.

2 Prepare the cake mix according to the package directions. Pour half of the batter into each pan.

3 Bake according to the package directions. Use an oven mitt or pot holder to remove the pans. Place cake pans on a wire cooling rack. Allow the cakes to cool for about 2 hours.

4 Slide a rubber scraper around the inside edges of the cake pans to loosen cakes. Cover the cake pans with the plates. Flip cakes upside down so they come out onto the plates.

5 Spread raspberry jam evenly across the top of one cake with the rubber scraper. Place the other cake on top of the jam.

6 Cover the sides and top of the cake with whipped topping.

7 Place pineapple rings on top of the cake. Add a cherry in the center of each ring.

13

Tasty Tip

To add even more color and flavor to your cake, add mandarin orange slices on top of the cake.

What's better than a chocolate chip cookie? A chocolate chip cookie with peanut butter chunks! These cookies are perfect when you need dessert on the go.

DIFFICULTY LEVEL: ★ ★ ☆
MAKES: 2 DOZEN
PREHEAT OVEN: 375° FAHRENHEIT

PEANUT CHUNK AND CHOCOLATE CHIP COOKIES

WHAT YOU NEED

●● *Ingredients*

1 cup (2 sticks) butter, softened
¾ cup sugar
¾ cup brown sugar
2 eggs
2 teaspoons vanilla extract
2½ cups flour
½ teaspoons salt
1 teaspoon baking soda
1½ cups semi-sweet chocolate chips
1½ cups mini peanut butter cups

●● *Tools*

large mixing bowl   rubber scraper   cutting board

butter knife   baking sheet   oven mitt

pot holder   spatula   wire cooling rack

1. In a large mixing bowl, cream butter, sugar, and brown sugar with a rubber scraper.

2. Add eggs and vanilla to the bowl and stir.

3. Add flour, salt, baking soda, and chocolate chips to butter mixture. Mix ingredients with the rubber scraper until combined.

4. On a cutting board, cut peanut butter cups in half with a butter knife. Gently fold in peanut butter cups with the rubber scraper.

6. Place 2-inch balls of dough on an ungreased baking sheet, about 2 inches apart.

7. Bake the cookies for 8–10 minutes. Use an oven mitt or pot holder to remove the baking sheet from the oven.

8. Use a spatula to carefully remove cookies from the baking sheet. Place cookies on a wire cooling rack.

Read It Right

Some ingredients look alike but have different uses. Be sure to read ingredient labels carefully. Baking soda and baking powder look the same. However, these ingredients work differently in recipes. Sugar and salt look similar too, but you wouldn't want to mix them up in a recipe.

You don't need to be in the middle of the woods to enjoy a campfire. These cookies look like mini campfires, but they will go like wildfire when you set them out.

CAMPFIRE COOKIES

WHAT YOU NEED

●● *Ingredients*

1 cup butterscotch chips
1 cup semi-sweet chocolate chips
1 (12-ounce) bag chow mein noodles
1 cup cinnamon candies or candy corn

●● *Tools*

microwave-safe bowl

mixing spoon

rubber scraper

wax paper

1 Put butterscotch chips and chocolate chips into a microwave-safe bowl. Microwave for 30 seconds and stir with a mixing spoon. Continue heating the chips for 30 seconds at a time and stirring until the chips are melted.

2 Add chow mein noodles to the melted chips. Mix together with a rubber scraper.

3 Lay out a sheet of wax paper on a table. Place 2-inch balls of the mixture onto the wax paper.

4 While the chocolate is still sticky, top each log with 3–4 pieces of cinnamon candies or candy corn.

5 Let the logs set for 15 minutes.

16

17

Tasty Tip

   Substitute small stick pretzels for the chow mein noodles. This will give the dessert a great combination of salty and sweet.

Originating from Italy, cannolis have a crispy, flaky outer shell wrapped around a creamy cheese filling. This recipe isn't Grandma's cannoli, but it tastes just as sweet.

DIFFICULTY LEVEL: ★ ★ ☆
SERVING SIZE: 10

HOLY CANNOLI

WHAT YOU NEED

●● *Ingredients*

1 (14-ounce) package cream cheese
²/₃ cup powdered sugar
2 teaspoons vanilla extract
¼ cup mini chocolate chips
10 sugar ice cream cones

●● *Tools*

large mixing bowl   electric mixer

rubber scraper

gallon-sized zip-top plastic bag

scissors

1 Put cream cheese in a large mixing bowl. Blend with an electric mixer on the cream setting for 8–10 minutes or until there are no lumps.

2 Add powdered sugar and vanilla to the bowl. Use the mixer to blend the ingredients together for 1 minute.

3 Add mini chocolate chips to the cream cheese mixture and stir with a rubber scraper.

4 Scoop the mixture into a zip-top plastic bag.

5 With a scissors, cut off a small hole in one corner of the bag.

6 Squeeze the mixture out of the hole in the zip-top bag and into the ice cream cones. Serve immediately or refrigerate.

Say Cheese

Cannolis are usually made with ricotta cheese. Ricotta is a soft, white cheese that is similar to cottage cheese. Ricotta or cream cheese can be used in this recipe. However, cream cheese is usually easier to find and costs less.

You already know ice cream is fun to eat. But did you also know it is fun to make? There's ice cream to be made, so grab a can and get shakin'.

DIFFICULTY LEVEL: ★ ★ ★
SERVING SIZE: 2-4

COFFEE CAN ICE CREAM

WHAT YOU NEED

● ● *Ingredients*

1 (16-ounce) carton heavy cream
½ cup sugar
1 tablespoon vanilla extract
7 to 8 cups crushed ice
1 cup rock salt

● ● *Tools*

large mixing bowl

whisk

1 small coffee can, empty and clean
1 large coffee can, empty and clean
duct tape

1 In a large mixing bowl, mix together the cream, sugar, and vanilla with a whisk for 30 seconds or until smooth.

2 Pour the mixture into a small coffee can. Put the lid on tight and wrap with duct tape to keep it shut.

3 Put the small can into a large can. Spread the crushed ice and rock salt around the outside of the small coffee can.

4 Put the lid on the large can and wrap with duct tape. Tip the can on its side and roll the can back and forth for 20 minutes.

5 After 20 minutes of rolling, open the cans to see if the ice cream has thickened. It should hold its shape and should not be runny.

6 If the ice cream is still runny, replace the small lid. Empty the melted ice and salt from the big can. Add fresh ice and salt. Roll the can for 5 minutes or until ice cream holds its shape.

Flavor Faves

You don't have to settle for plain vanilla ice cream. You can make your favorite flavor by adding a few simple ingredients.

- For strawberry ice cream, add ½ cup sliced strawberries in step 1. Continue with steps 2–6.

- To make mint chocolate chip ice cream, just replace the vanilla extract with mint extract in step 1. Add ½ cup mini chocolate chips. Continue with steps 2–6.

When you're in need of some serious chocolate, this dessert hits the spot. Chocolate Cherry Brownies combine two sweet flavors into one rich treat. Get ready for a chocolate blast!

DIFFICULTY LEVEL: ★ ★ ☆
SERVING SIZE: 18–24
PREHEAT OVEN: 350° FAHRENHEIT

CHOCOLATE CHERRY BROWNIES

WHAT YOU NEED

•• Ingredients

4 squares unsweetened baking chocolate
¾ cup butter, softened
2 cups sugar
3 eggs
1½ teaspoons vanilla extract
1½ cups flour
1 teaspoon baking powder
½ teaspoons salt
1 (21-ounce) can cherry pie filling
1 cup chocolate chips

•• Tools

microwave-safe bowl   rubber scraper   9 x 13 baking pan

oven mitt   pot holder   wire cooling rack

nonstick cooking spray

1 In a microwave-safe bowl, microwave chocolate squares and butter on high for 2 minutes.

2 Remove bowl from the microwave and stir mixture with a rubber scraper. Microwave for another 30 seconds to completely melt the chocolate.

3 Add sugar, eggs, and vanilla to chocolate mixture and stir. Mix in flour, baking powder, and salt. Stir with the rubber scraper until combined.

5 Spray a 9 x 13 baking pan with nonstick cooking spray. Pour batter into the pan. Bake for 35 minutes.

6 Use an oven mitt or pot holder to remove brownies from the oven. Set the pan on a wire cooling rack. When cool, spread cherry pie filling on top of brownies.

7 Place chocolate chips in the microwave-safe bowl. Microwave for 30 seconds and stir with the rubber scraper. Microwave for another 30 seconds or until chips are completely melted. Drizzle melted chocolate on top of brownies.

Add the Finishing Touch

Want to dress up your brownies a bit? Here are a few tips to give your brownies some extra flair:

• Add a dusting of powdered sugar. Place ½ cup powdered sugar into a flour sifter. Sprinkle sugar on top of the brownies.

• Mix 1 cup pecans and 1 cup chopped walnuts into the batter for a nutty flavor.

Pecan pie is a classic holiday dessert. Turtle sundaes are yummy treats. With this Turtle Sundae Pecan Pie, you get the best of both.

DIFFICULTY LEVEL: ★ ★ ★
SERVING SIZE: 8–10
PREHEAT OVEN: 375° FAHRENHEIT

TURTLE SUNDAE PECAN PIE

WHAT YOU NEED

•• Ingredients

3 tablespoons butter
3 eggs
1 cup dark corn syrup
1 cup sugar
2 teaspoons vanilla extract
1 refrigerated piecrust
1¼ cup pecan halves
1 spray can or tub whipped topping
1 jar caramel ice cream topping
1 cup mini chocolate chips

•• Tools

 microwave-safe bowl

 large mixing bowl

 whisk

 pie pan   baking sheet

 oven mitt

 pot holder

1 Put butter into a microwave-safe bowl and microwave for 30 seconds or until butter is completely melted. Pour butter into a large mixing bowl.

2 Add eggs, dark corn syrup, sugar, and vanilla to the mixing bowl. Combine ingredients with a whisk.

3 Press piecrust into a pie pan. Evenly cover piecrust with pecans. Pour egg mixture over pecans.

4 Place the pie pan on a baking sheet and bake for 50 minutes.

5 Use an oven mitt or pot holder to carefully remove the pie from the oven. Let it cool for 1 hour.

6 When cool, decorate the top of the pie with whipped topping. Drizzle caramel ice cream topping and mini chocolate chips on top.

Lighten Up

If you don't have dark corn syrup on hand, you can use light corn syrup. Just use brown sugar in place of regular sugar.

In a Nutshell

The world's largest pecan is located in Brunswick, Missouri. The nut is made out of concrete and weighs more than 12,000 pounds!

This Tremendous Triple Berry Trifle is full of fresh berries and bright colors. It is perfect when you need a cool treat on a hot day.

DIFFICULTY LEVEL: ★ ☆ ☆
SERVING SIZE: 8–10

TREMENDOUS TRIPLE BERRY TRIFLE

WHAT YOU NEED

● ● *Ingredients*

1 pint raspberries
1 pint blueberries
1 pint blackberries
2 tablespoons lemon juice
½ cup sugar
1 package sugar wafer cookies
1 (12-ounce) container whipped topping

● ● *Tools*

large mixing bowl

mixing spoon

trifle bowl
or serving dish

butter knife

1 In a large mixing bowl, add berries, lemon juice, and sugar. Fold ingredients together with a mixing spoon, being careful not to smash the berries.

2 Cover the bottom of a trifle bowl or serving dish with a layer of cookies.

3 Spread ½ cup whipped topping evenly on top of cookies with a butter knife.

4 Spread ⅓ of the berry mixture over the whipped topping.

5 Continue to add layers of cookies, whipped topping, and berries until dish is full.

6 Arrange the remaining fruit on top of the whipped topping in a fun design. Chill in the refrigerator for 30 minutes before serving.

Tasty Tip

Feeling adventurous? Try using different fruits. Build your trifle with slices of kiwi, banana, and fresh strawberries. You can mix these fruits with the berries for even more flavor. Mix and match to come up with yummy fruit flavors.

TOOLS GLOSSARY

9 x 13 baking pan — a glass or metal pan used to cook food

baking sheet — a flat metal tray used for baking foods

butter knife — an eating utensil often used to spread ingredients

cake pan — a glass or metal pan used for baking cakes

cutting board — a wooden or plastic board used when slicing or chopping foods

electric mixer — a hand-held or stand-based mixer that uses rotating beaters to mix ingredients

microwave-safe bowl — a non-metal bowl used in microwave ovens

mixing bowl — a sturdy bowl used for mixing ingredients

mixing spoon — a large spoon with a wide, circular end used to mix ingredients

oven mitt — a large mitten made from heavy fabric used to protect hands when removing hot pans from the oven

paring knife — a small, sharp knife used for peeling or slicing

pie pan — a glass or metal pan used for baking pies

pizza cutter — a round knife that spins on a handle as you slice

pizza pan — a circular pan that is used for baking pizza

pot holder — a thick, heavy fabric cut into a square or circle that is used to remove hot pans from an oven

rolling mat — a flat, plastic surface used when rolling out dough

rolling pin — a cylinder-shaped tool used to flatten dough

rubber scraper — a kitchen tool with a rubber paddle on the end

small bowl — a bowl used for mixing a small amount of ingredients

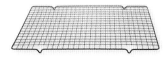

spatula — a kitchen tool with a broad, flat metal or plastic blade at the end, used for removing food from a pan

trifle bowl — a clear, glass bowl with tall sides used to serve layered food

whisk— a metal tool used for beating ingredients

wire cooling rack — a rectangular rack that allows baked goods to cool quickly and evenly

GLOSSARY

cannoli (kan-OH-lee) — Italian pastry made from tube-shaped pastry shells filled with ricotta cheese or whipped cream

cream (KREEM) — to mix ingredients until soft and smooth

drizzle (DRIZ-uhl) — to let a substance fall in small drops

extract (EK-strakt) — a solid or liquid concentrate solution or plant juice; vanilla extract is made from vanilla beans.

fold (FOHLD) — to mix or add ingredients by gently turning the light ingredient over the heavy ingredient

substitute (SUHB-stuh-toot) — something used in place of another

trifle (TRYE-fuhl) — a layered dessert usually made with custard, cake, and fruit

READ MORE

Carle, Megan, Jill Carle, and Judi Carle. *Teens Cook Dessert.* Berkeley: Ten Speed Press, 2006.

Ibbs, Katharine. *I Can Cook!* New York: DK, 2007.

Larrew, Brekka Hervey. *Apple Pie Calzones and Other Cookie Recipes.* Fun Food for Cool Cooks. Mankato, Minn.: Capstone Press, 2008.

INTERNET SITES

FactHound offers a safe, fun way to find Internet sites related to this book. All of the sites on FactHound have been researched by our staff.

Here's how:
1. Visit *www.facthound.com*
2. Choose your grade level.
3. Type in this book ID **1429613378** for age-appropriate sites. You may also browse subjects by clicking on letters, or by clicking on pictures and words.
4. Click on the **Fetch It** button.

FactHound will fetch the best sites for you!

ABOUT THE AUTHOR

Kristi Johnson got her start in the kitchen when she was a little girl helping her mom, aunt, and grandmas with cooking and baking. Over the years, she decided that her true passion was in baking. She spent many days in the kitchen covering every countertop with her favorite chocolate chip cookies.

Kristi attended the baking program at the Le Cordon Bleu College of Culinary Arts in Minnesota. After graduating with highest honors, Kristi worked in many restaurants and currently works in the baking industry.

INDEX